Reading for sion
C

Teachers' notes

Introduction

This book contains activity sheets for sequencing and cloze procedure. It is intended for children working at Key Stage 2.

These activities are not designed as teaching tools in themselves, but rather they offer children practice in newly acquired skills. In order that children gain the maximum benefit from these activities, it is essential that they are incorporated into a learning environment which offers time for talking, listening, thinking, telling, reading and writing.

There is always a danger with photocopiable sheets that children will see them simply as time-fillers. Always explain the purpose of the activity so that they concentrate on that aspect of the task.

Aims of this book

- To encourage reading for meaning.
- To help children to see logical connections within texts.
- To focus upon particular parts of speech.
- To assist children in constructing coherent writing.

Sequencing

Sequencing activities present children with sections of text which are not in the correct order which they are then required to reorder into a sensible sequence. Such activities promote logical thinking and encourage children to pay careful attention to the precise meaning of the text in front of them.

These tasks demand a broken, reflective read and the children need to consider each section before completing the organisation of the whole text. This is important as many children who have acquired initial fluency in reading can become over-casual, particularly when reading fiction. They are content to extract just the gist of a story and fail to attend to any more subtle meanings. Tasks which require them to fully comprehend all aspects of the text are an important means by which they can become familiar with the essentials of successful reading – the persistent search for meaning.

Demonstrate a sequencing activity before asking the children to complete a particular task. It is suggested that they undertake the sequencing tasks in pairs, as the resulting discussion about the order of the text often confirms the learning. The children have to justify their choices to one another and this consolidates their knowledge. Discussing together why a certain piece of text cannot follow another, helps them to understand the causal connections in texts. Sometimes children are asked to work in pairs but, in fact, work as two individuals sitting close to one another! Giving each pair only one copy of the sequencing sheet can result in profitable discussion and negotiation of answers.

Page 32 is a blank master sheet for use with some of the sequencing activities. You will need to provide blank paper for the others.The children should cut up each text page as indicated and then stick the strips of text on to the blank sections. Tell the children to position the text in what they believe to be the right order and then to reread the whole text to check for continuity before fixing the text in place.

Cloze procedure

Cloze procedure was originally devised as a means of assessing the readability of a text. It is now widely used as a means of assessing the extent to which a reader has fully comprehended a text.

The text is presented with gaps and the children must read attentively in order to make accurate predictions about which words would fill the gaps. When children complete the deletions, they bring their own language and knowledge to reading the text. Thus, it becomes more meaningful and important to them. Cloze procedure tasks generate a considerable amount of thinking about a text and they also encourage prediction, as the child is required to read ahead to seek justification for the word selected to fill the gap.

The children should be encouraged to read the whole text (or at least the whole sentence) before inserting a missing word. Often a clue to the most accurate word lies in text which follows the gap. This encourages children to see the fluency of writing and the continuity of texts.

Remind the children that cloze deletions do not necessarily have only one correct response. Tell them to jot down in rough all their suggestions and then decide which is the most appropriate, trying to be sensitive to the style of the author. Children usually like to compare their 'answers' with the ones provided and this checking and comparing can become part of the learning process. Discuss why their particular word, although appropriate, might not be as good as the one provided in the answers. Similarly, encourage them to defend their choice of word. All of this negotiation heightens children's awareness of the appropriacy of language.

All children, but particularly hesitant spellers, should be reassured that exciting words are valued and that spelling can always be checked once the most suitable word has been selected.

It can often be valuable to organise the children into pairs of mixed ability. The weaker reader has support for the reading of the text and the more able reader may have to explain their reasons for suggesting any particular word. This 'teaching' is a very effective way of learning.

There are different types of cloze procedure. Some passages have 'random deletions'. This means that words have been deleted in a regular cycle, for example, every ninth word. This kind of cloze is used on pages 11–13, where the activities are graded in difficulty. There are deletions approximately every ninth or tenth word in the easiest activity and every seventh or eighth word for the most difficult. Other cloze activities are based on 'specific deletions'. This means that specific vocabulary has been deleted to encourage the child to reuse particular aspects of language. For example, in a non-fiction text it can be very useful to delete new technical vocabulary as a means of checking whether the child has absorbed its meaning. Specific deletions can also be applied to parts of speech to encourage children to concentrate upon specific tools of language, for example adjectives, verbs or adverbs. The activities in this book offer practice in all kinds of specific deletions.

Pointing out that the length of the line does not indicate the length of the deleted word.

Children often assume that the word deleted must be an 'important' word and this means that they are not expecting the word to be 'on', 'in' or 'by'. Remind them that these little words also have an important part to play in the cohesive construction of a text.

Notes on individual activities

Pages 5–10: Cloze and sequencing

These activities are arranged in linked pairs. This means, for example, that there is a cloze activity followed by a sequencing activity both on the topic of the Romans. These dual tasks avoid what can otherwise be the isolated nature of such activities. The children can take their interest in one activity forward into the next. Each sequencing activity is only broadly linked with its related cloze activity, but it helps children to appreciate how knowledge is interconnected. The deletions are every ninth or tenth word giving children a range of words to supply. Give the children copies of the blank master sheet (page 32) to fit the sequenced text into whenever appropriate.

Answers

Page 5 sequenced order: 3, 2, 1, 4, 6, 5.
Page 6 missing words: Romans, more, people, in, lines, horse, one, street, the, in, took, meet, was.
Page 7 sequenced order: 3, 2, 1, 6, 4, 5.

Page 8 missing words: burning, window, terrifying, to, other, our, frightened, was, both, and, packed, held.
Page 9 sequenced order: 3, 1, 6, 4, 2, 5.
Page 10 missing words: carried, We, in, train, seat, one, helped, held, We, arm, sprang, soldiers, heard, brother.

Pages 11–13: Cloze – newspaper articles

These cloze activities are presented as newspaper-style articles. When completing a cloze passage it is important that children are sensitive to the style and genre of the passage. Newspaper reports, for example, have a particular journalistic style.

Answers

Page 11 missing words: be, popular, coconut, It, be, will, There, out, excitement, likely, very, Sale, catch, delicious, young.
Page 12 missing words: to, spot, really, match, minute, defence, but, the, missed, It, after, almost, ecstatic, hope.
Page 13 missing words: fast, nesting, are, to, houses, if, came, the, set, barn, other, would, sure, the, supplying, over, place, help.

Pages 14–18: Poetry sequencing

These activities require the children to reorder lines from poems. The first poem does not rhyme. The children will have to follow the humorous logic of the lines to sequence the poem. The first line has been indicated. The subsequent poems are graded in difficulty. It is worth pointing out to the children that the poem 'Robin sang sweetly' can begin with lines about summer or with lines about autumn. Ask the children which they prefer and why. Does the chosen beginning affect the poem? The most challenging activity is 'The thrushes' nest'. Advise the children to look carefully at the rhyming pattern. As the rhyming sequence is more complex it is difficult to predict the sequence. It might be appropriate to give some pairs the starting lines for this poem. Encourage them to learn the poems by heart.

Answers

Page 14 sequenced order: 1, 8, 4, 11, 5, 10, 2, 7, 3, 9, 6.
Page 15 sequenced order: 3, 1, 4, 6, 2, 5.
Page 16 sequenced order: 4, 2, 6, 1, 5, 3.
Page 17 sequenced order: 3, 7, 6, 4, 2, 8, 5, 1.
Page 18 sequenced order: 1, 3, 6, 2, 7, 5, 4.

Pages 19–21: Cloze – story passages

These activities are all based around well-known children's fiction. In the first activity, 'A pony and trap ride' (from *The Secret Garden*), all the deletions are of verbs. In 'Wild cherries' (from *The Railway Children*), all the deletions are of adjectives. In 'Holiday at sea' (from *Swallows and Amazons*), all the deletions are of adverbs. Before the children undertake these activities, it is essential to check that they are familiar with these parts of speech. It is also interesting to note that with these specific deletions there are always more variations of words that fit semantically into the gaps. Encourage the children to make lists of these words before completing the photocopiable page and to decide which word they prefer.

Answers

Page 19 missing words: arrived, was, discover, curled, kept, cast, caught, drove, saw, passed, noticed, began, were, hear.
Page 20 missing words: sunny, beautiful, wild, steep, young, large, white, old, ripe, precious, great, empty.
Page 21 missing words: tidily, gently, slowly, quickly, excitedly, steadily, loudly, eagerly, happily, uncontrollably, wearily.

Pages 22–24: Sequencing – traditional tales

These activities are based around well-known stories ('The musicians of Bremen', 'The elves and the shoemaker', 'The fisherman and his wife') which should help the children with the task of sequencing the text. Since these tales should be familiar taleto the children, the extracts of text in each section are quite long.

Extension activity

Ask the children to work in pairs to write out a well-known story. Then tell them to cut up the stories into six or seven sections and ask other children to resequence them. The children will initially need help in writing the tale with enough clues as to the next episode. Encourage them to think of the story in separate paragraphs and to write it out with clear spaces between each section as this will make it easier for the children who are to resequence the story.

Answers

Page 22 sequenced order: 3, 1, 6, 4, 2, 5.
Page 23 sequenced order: 5, 3, 2, 6, 1, 4.
Page 24 sequenced order: 4, 1, 5, 3, 6, 2.

Pages 25–27: Information and cloze

These activities are all based around the theme 'Discoveries'. The task is different from the previous cloze passages in which the children are expected to complete the gaps drawing upon their own language knowledge. In these activities, the deletions are content words specific to the topic and so the children are expected to read the passage at the top of the page carefully and then to use the new vocabulary from it to complete the cloze passage in the lower half of the page. This encourages children to read information in a more deliberate and thoughtful way.

Answers

Page 25 missing words: young, Howard Carter, important, four, throne, gold, clothing, Egypt, greatest.
Page 26 missing words: 1982, sea, spectacular, world, sank, VIII, French, successful, preserved.
Page 27 missing words: 1905, spinning, gyroscope, axis, movement, gyroscope, 1908, navigation.

Pages 28–32: Sequencing instructions and directions

These activities give children practice in presenting a set of instructions in the correct order. This is a skill which some children find particularly difficult. They may be aware of the things that need to be done in order to complete a task but they are uncertain about the precise sequence of events. These activities also give children the opportunity to handle the particular ways in which we present instructions using the imperative form of the verb; that is, 'add', 'turn', 'sift' and so on.

Extension activity

Encourage the children to devise their own maps. They should provide a clear set of instructions to help another pair to reach an objective; for example they could draw a treasure map with gold hidden somewhere or a map of the school and give directions to a certain room.

National Curriculum: English

These activities support the following requirements of the National Curriculum for English.

Programme of study for reading
Key Stage 2
10. Pupils should:
- be encouraged to think about the accuracy of their own reading and check for errors that distort meaning.

Statements of attainment
AT2 – Pupils should be able to:
(3e) bring to their writing and discussion about stories some understanding of the way stories are structured.
(4c) demonstrate, in talking about stories, poems, non-fiction and other texts, that they are developing their abilities to use inference, deduction and previous reading experience.

AT3 – Pupils should be able to:
(4a) produce, independently, pieces of writing showing evidence of a developing ability to structure what is written in ways that make the meaning clear to the reader;....
(4c) organise non-chronological writing for different purposes in orderly ways.
(5e) show in discussion the ability to recognise variations in vocabulary according to purpose, topic and audience....

Scottish 5–14 Curriculum: English Language

Attainment outcome	Strand	Attainment target	Level
Reading	Reading for information	Find and use information specific to their needs from a range of informational and reference sources.	C
	Reading to reflect on the writer's ideas and craft	Read a variety of texts and show they understand the main ideas and can draw conclusions from the text.	C
	Awareness of genre	Identify a few obvious features of form and content in different types of text: stories, poems, dramatic texts, newspaper items, informational and reference texts.	C
	Knowledge about language	Show they know, understand and can use the terms: fiction, non-fiction, verse, paragraph.	C

● Name ____________________________

The Roman invasion of Britain

After their defeat in 50 BC, the Britons promised to pay money to Rome and stop supporting the Gauls. Consequently, the Romans sailed away, only to return 100 years later.

Caesar wanted to punish the Britons for supporting the Gauls, so he sailed across the Channel. His army defeated the Britons in a fierce fight on the beach.

In 50 BC the Britons were helping their allies, the Gauls, to fight against the Roman Empire. The Romans were led by a famous general called Julius Caesar.

So a hundred years later, in AD 50, the Romans returned to conquer Britain. They wanted to make it part of the powerful Roman Empire.

Finally, the Britons had to accept defeat. The Romans continued to rule most of Britain for nearly 400 years.

The Britons fought bravely, led by their chief whose name was Caractacus. However, the Roman army was stronger, better trained and well organised.

● Name ______________________________

A Roman town

When the Romans came to Britain there were no real towns or ports, just villages and settlements.

As in all other parts of their empire, the ________________ set to work to build towns. It was ________________ civilised, easier to collect taxes and enforce laws if ________________ lived in towns.

A Roman town was set out ________________ an orderly way. The streets crossed each other in straight ________________. The main streets were paved and wide enough for a ________________ and cart to pass. There were stepping stones connecting ________________ pavement to another.

Small shops lined the main ________________, but the Roman slaves did most of the shopping in ________________ market-place or forum. The forum was a wide, open space ________________ the centre of the town. Public meetings ________________ place there. Most towns had public baths where people would ________________, not only to wash but also to meet friends. There ________________ often a theatre for plays and sporting events.

You can still see evidence of the Roman occupation in many towns and cities in Britain today.

● Name ______________________

The Great Fire of London

✂

The Lord Mayor ordered houses to be pulled down to check the path of the fire. This did not work as the fire overtook their attempts.

At that time, houses were built very close together and many of the houses were made of wood. They burned easily and helped the fire to spread quickly.

The Great Fire of London started in a baker's shop in Pudding Lane. The year was 1666. The fire quickly spread through the city, destroying many churches including St Paul's Cathedral.

Finally, groups of sailors blew up houses with gunpowder which was much quicker. The wider gaps eventually stopped the spread of the fire.

London was rebuilt within six years. Houses were built of brick and stone and streets were wider and cleaner. Sir Christopher Wren rebuilt St Paul's Cathedral which can be seen today.

When the houses were pulled down, the terrified people fled to the River Thames with what belongings they could salvage. They jumped into boats hoping to cross the river to safety.

● Name ____________________________

Fleeing to safety – an extract from a child's diary

We had gone to bed early that particular day. My mother and father had guests and were dining late.

I woke suddenly. I was aware of a strong smell of ________________.

I rushed out of bed and looked out of the high casement ________________.

A scene of great confusion met my eyes.

Most ________________ of all was a long line of flames that seemed ________________ stretch from one end of London to the ________________. It lit up the sky and was advancing towards ________________ house. Both the cracking of the flaming timbers and the ________________ shouts of the people in the streets below added to the chaos.

My father, who ________________ white and shaken, woke my sister and hurried us ________________ downstairs. My mother tied damp cloths over our mouths ________________ took us out to a cart which was already ________________ with our belongings.

When we were finally in the boat, crossing the Thames to safety, I looked back. I ________________ my sister's hand and smiled at my exhausted parents. At least my family were safe. September 2nd 1666, I knew, was a night I would never forget.

Name ______________________

A wartime memory

I had to make sure that my brother was awake. He used to be very bad-tempered if he was disturbed in the night and he wanted to go back to sleep.

The Andersen shelter was dug into the ground. It had no heating and it always felt cold. My brother always used to grab the top bunk. There was often a puddle of rainwater on the rough cement floor.

If we heard the air-raid siren in the night we had to get up and put on warm clothes over our night things. We had to wear our shoes because it was often wet as we walked down the garden.

Mum used to hurry us down the garden path to the Andersen shelter. We weren't allowed to use a light so we often bumped into things. My dad was not with us. He was a soldier and we didn't even know where he was.

We could hear the planes going overhead and the thud of guns, but mum used to tell us not to worry. We would fall asleep and stay in the Andersen shelter until morning.

The twins, who were only babies, had to be put in the wicker laundry basket. They didn't even wake up. They had a stone hot-water bottle, wrapped in a blanket, to help keep them warm.

● Name ______________________________

A wartime journey

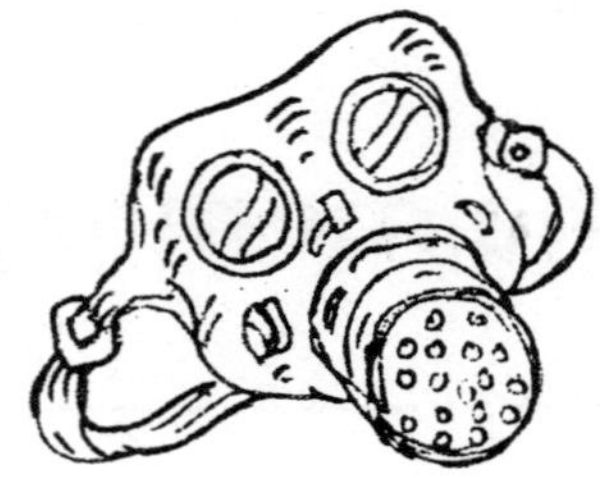

It was cold. The station was crowded. It was bustling with soldiers with kitbags, wailing children, engines steaming gently and noise everywhere.

Everyone ________________ a gas mask case. I was lucky that I was with my mum and my brothers. ________________ were leaving London to stay with an aunt ________________ a safe part of the country.

The ________________ was in the station and everyone surged forward to try and get a ________________ on the train. My mum had my baby brother in ________________ arm and a large suitcase in the other. A soldier took the suitcase and ________________ her to a seat in the carriage. I carried the baby's food and our sandwiches and ________________ tightly to my mum's coat.

The train was full. ________________ heard the whistle blow. My mother clutched my ________________. Where was John? My heart missed a beat. I ________________ up and pushed my way into the corridor shouting 'John! John!' I couldn't get past the ________________. I was crying now. Suddenly I ________________ an embarrassed shout, 'I'm here!' It was my ________________, he was on the train. I went back into the carriage and smiled at my mum through my tears. It was all right, we were still all together.

● Name ________________________

Morley Fun Day

On Saturday 9 August, from midday until late, there will be a Fun Day in Morley. It will be held on the playing field of Richard Morley Primary School.

There will ______________ lots of activities taking place including the immensely ______________ 'Welly throwing'. You can try your luck at the ______________ shy or maybe have a go at skittles. ______________ looks easy, doesn't it?

The highlight, of course, will ______________ the incredible spectacle of ferret racing, and there ______________ be an opportunity to bet on the winner. ______________ will be local school teams battling it ______________ in five-a-side football which always brings ______________ to the supporters. Young visitors are more ______________ to get excited about the bouncy castle – a ______________ popular feature.

Take a look at the Car Boot ______________, there is a chance of a bargain here! Use the Fun Day to see your friends, ______________ up on the gossip and perhaps try one of Mrs Reid's ______________ cakes as well.

Morley Fun Day promises to be a great day out for ______________ and old alike. Don't forget, 9 August, BE THERE!

● Name ________________________________

Football report

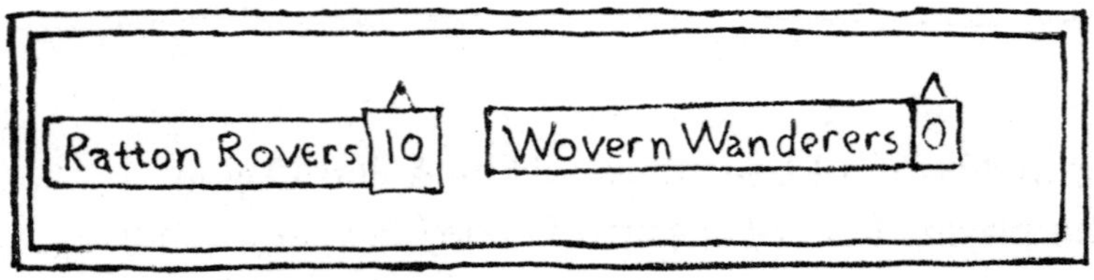

What a match! What a disaster! With last season's top scorer failing a late fitness test, Wovern Wanderers could only field a team of ten.

The first corner of the game went ________________ Wanderers, but it was the only high ________________. They lost their way in spite of working ________________ hard to compensate for the missing striker. The miss of the ________________ came in the tenth ________________ when Towner raced clear of Rover's ________________. Smith raced out to try and intercept, ________________ Towner rounded him with ease. He approached ________________ net with not another player near, took aim and ________________! The groans echoed around the Wovern football ground. ________________ was downhill from then on. Goal ________________ goal until the tenth was received in ________________ total silence by the Wovern supporters and ________________ joy by visiting Rovers.

The Wanderers must ________________ for a quick recovery by Ken Watchen. Next week can only be better!

● Name ______________________________

The Hoot and Screech Club

READ THIS, IT'S IMPORTANT!

Hi! I'm Harold Hoot. Did you know that owls in Britain are having a hard time of it?

Their traditional nesting sites are disappearing ________________. Woodland is being chopped down so ________________ in hollow trees becomes tricky. Barns ________________ being converted into houses or razed ________________ the ground to make way for ________________ and roads. How would you feel ________________ you were an owl and when it ________________ to nesting-time and you fancied ________________ same home as last year, you ________________ off, and when you arrived the ________________ had gone and there were no ________________ suitable homes for miles around? It ________________ put you right off laying, I'm ________________.

So, how can you help? Well ________________ Hoot and Screech Club are ________________ nesting boxes for suitable sites all ______________________ Britain. If you know of a ________________ where an owl could nest, or want to ________________ in any way get in touch with this club. The address is on the back page of the paper.

Remember – an owl in a nest,
an owl has a rest.

● Name ____________________

Why are fire engines red?

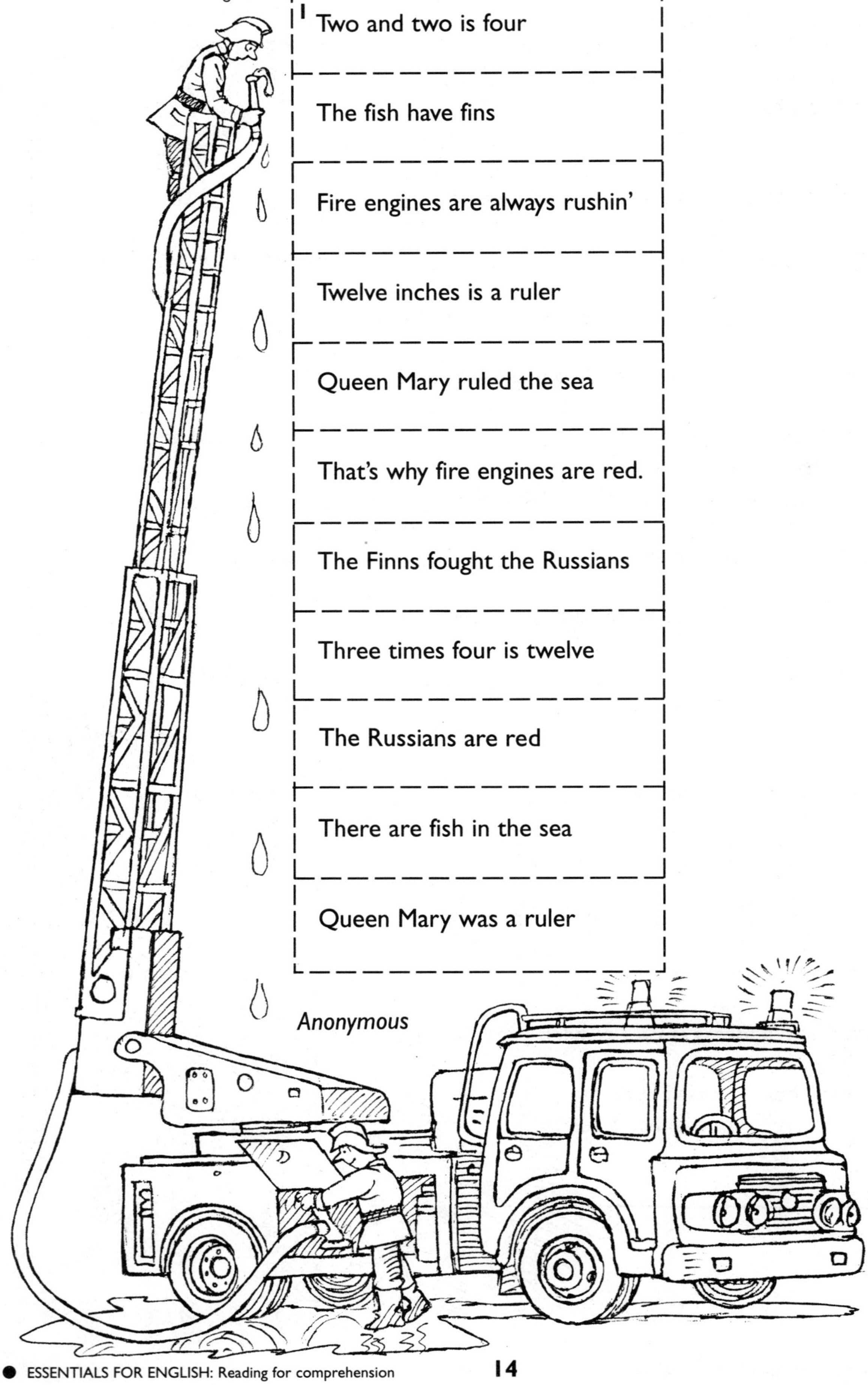

1 Two and two is four

The fish have fins

Fire engines are always rushin'

Twelve inches is a ruler

Queen Mary ruled the sea

That's why fire engines are red.

The Finns fought the Russians

Three times four is twelve

The Russians are red

There are fish in the sea

Queen Mary was a ruler

Anonymous

Name ______________________________

King Arthur

✂

He stole three sacks of barley meal
To make a bag-pudding.

The king and queen sat down to dine,
And all the court beside;

1

When good King Arthur ruled the land,
He was a goodly king;

A bag-pudding the queen did bake,
And stuffed it full of plums,

And what they could not eat that night,
The queen next morning fried.

And in it put great lumps of fat,
As big as my two thumbs.

Anonymous

● Name ______________________________

It's school today

✂

I wave to Mum and shut the gate I'll have to hurry it's half-past eight.
I wash my face, I brush my hair, I hang my nightdress on the chair.
I reach the gate: it's five to nine. Goodness me! I'm just in time.
I I wake up early, it's school today, I'll get up early and be on my way.
The bus has gone, I'll run to school. I pass the shops and the swimming pool.
The breakfast table is all set, I'll eat it quickly and feed my pet.

Anonymous

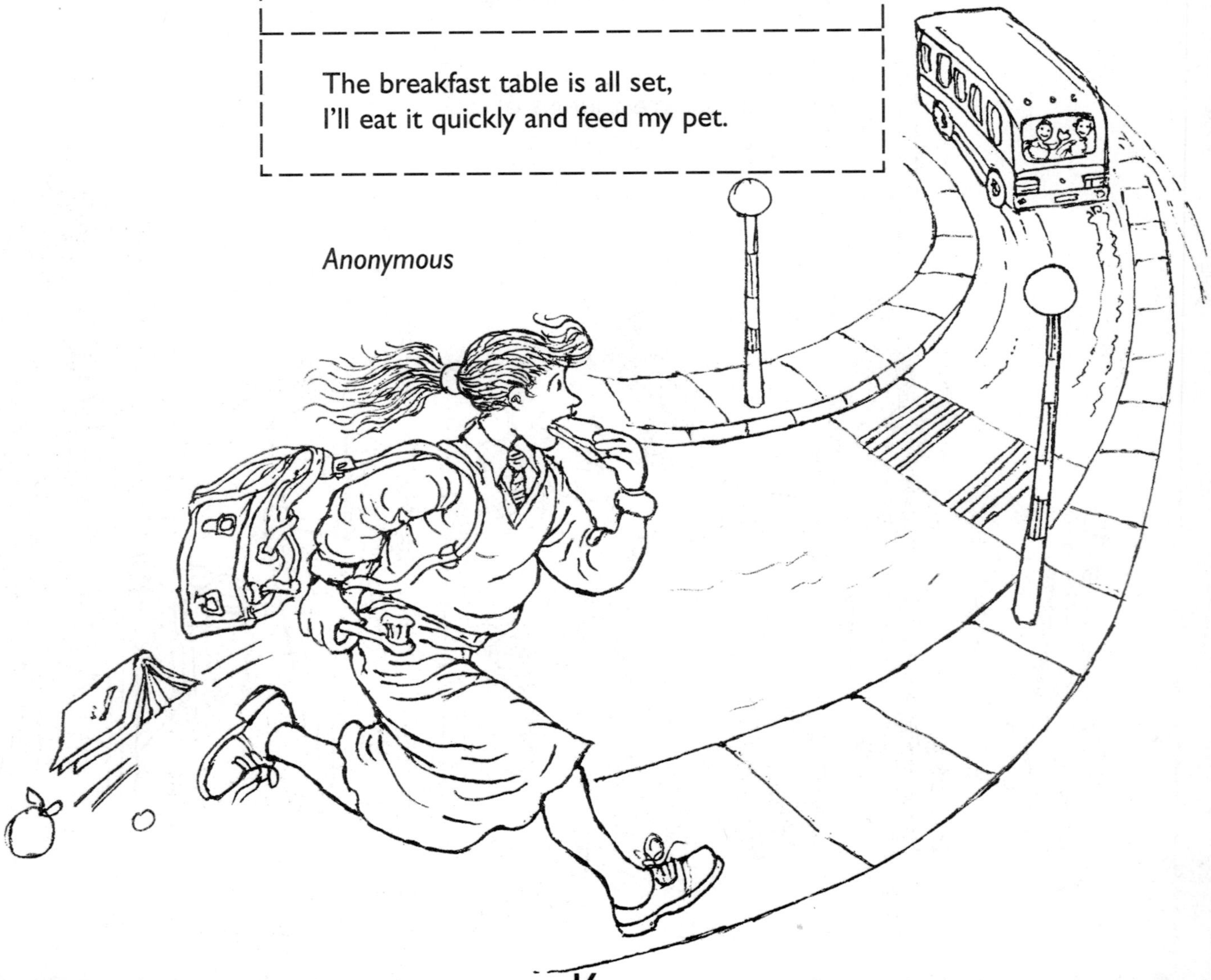

● Name ______________________

Robin sang sweetly

When the spring came back again,
He sang, 'I told you so!'

In the cold and wintry weather
Still you hear his song.

Robin sang sweetly
When the days were bright.

'There are fruits for everyone.
Let us all give praise!'

Keep on singing through the winter;
'It will always go.'

Robin sang sweetly
In the autumn days:

'Thanks! Thanks for summer!'
He sang with all his might.

'Somebody must sing,' said Robin,
'Or winter will seem long.'

Anonymous

Name ______________________________

The thrushes' nest

(This poem, by John Clare, was written over a hundred years ago.)

✂

1

Within a thick and spreading hawthorn bush
That overhung a molehill large and round,

How true she warped the moss to form a nest,
And modelled it with in the wood and clay;

I heard from morn to morn a merry thrush
Sing hymns to sunrise, and I drank the sound.

A brood of nature's minstrels chirp and fly
Glad as that sunshine and the laughing sky.

Ink spotted over shells of greeny blue;
And there I witnessed, in the sunny hours,

With joy; and, often an intruding guest,
I watched her secret toils from day to day –

And by and by, like heath bells gilt with dew,
There lay her shining eggs, as bright as flowers,

● Name ______________________________

A pony and trap ride

Mary is going on holiday to stay with an aunt and uncle whom she has never met. They live on the edge of a wild moor.

It was late at night when Mary ________________ at the station and the wind was howling. She ________________ surprised to ________________ that the remainder of her journey was by pony and trap.

Mary ________________ up in the corner of the trap and ________________ her eyes on the road ahead. The lamps on the trap ________________ rays of light a little distance ahead. Mary ________________ fleeting glimpses of the things they passed.

They ________________ through a tiny village and she ________________ whitewashed cottages and the lights of a public house. They ________________ an ancient church and a large vicarage. She ________________ the lights of a shop window. Then the village was gone.

At last the trotting horses ________________ to go more slowly, as if they ________________ climbing a steep hill. She could see nothing now but a wall of darkness on either side of the trap. She could ________________ the panting of the horses. She leaned forward, the trap gave an enormous jolt and lurched to a stop. They were there.

● Name ______________________________

Wild cherries

A long time ago three children lived in a small cottage in the country. They were very poor and were searching for a present for their mother who was recovering from an illness.

Wild cherries! This idea occurred to the children when they woke up that ________________ morning. They had seen the ________________ blossom on the trees in the spring and knew where to look for ________________ cherries now that cherry-time was here.

Many trees grew along the ________________ bank of the river which the ________________ children were not allowed to climb.

There were all sorts of trees growing there. Birches and beeches and ________________ oaks and hazels and among them the ________________ blossom shone like snow.

Mother had let them take their lunch in an ________________ basket. It would do to carry the ________________ cherries back in; if they found any. Mother also lent them her ________________ silver watch so that they would not be late for tea.

With ________________ care the children picked the cherries. They all tried to reach the cherries at the ends of the branches. Soon they had filled the ________________ basket and they carried it triumphantly home.

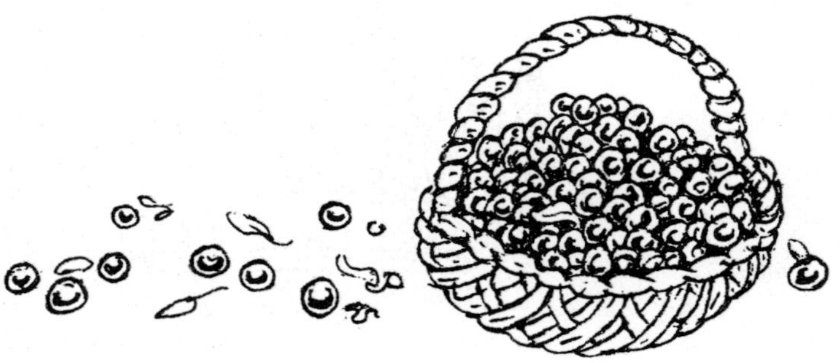

● Name ______________________________

Holiday at sea

John and Wendy climbed down the steps into the noisy and bustling harbour. The sun shone brightly and there wasn't a cloud in the sky.

This was the first day of their first ever sailing holiday. They grinned at each other. They were excited. The luggage had to be stowed ________________ in the cabin because there wasn't much room. It wasn't a very big boat. The wind was blowing ________________ and they could feel the boat moving ________________ against the harbour wall.

The children had been told they could go down to the beach for a swim. They ________________ put on their swimming costumes, left the boat and ran ________________ to the nearby beach.

John looked at the waves, rolling ________________ down the beach. He shouted ________________ to Wendy and jumped ________________ into the waves. They were so strong that he struggled to keep his balance. Then Wendy ran into the sea and, holding John's hand, they jumped ________________ in the waves.

Eventually the sun went in. John began to shiver ________________ and they both grabbed their towels. They clambered ________________ back to the boat.

Dinner was ready. Tomorrow they would set sail. Then, the holiday would really begin!

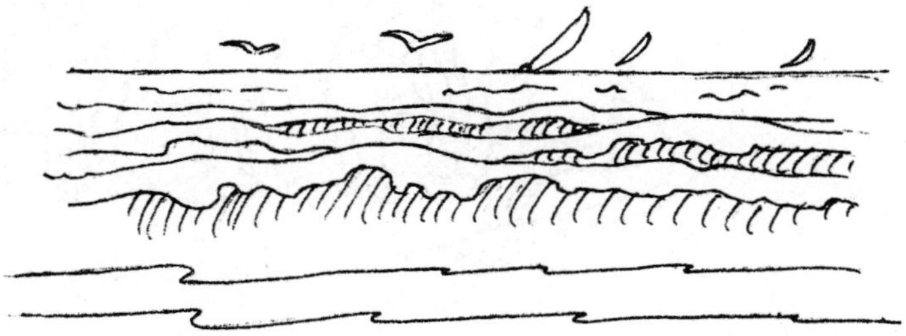

● Name ______________________

The travelling musicians

They came across a house in which a band of robbers were feasting, so the animals practised their music. The ass brayed loudly, the dog barked fiercely, the cat meowed shrilly and the cock crowed hoarsely.

The robber thought a witch with long bony fingers had scratched his face, a man with a knife had stabbed him in the leg, a monster had hit him with a club and a devil was shouting at him from above.

An old ass, a dog, a cat and a cockerel, no longer wanted by their owners, decided to set off to the city to become musicians.

When all was dark, one brave robber came back. However, the cat scratched and spat at him and the dog bit him in the leg. The ass kicked him and the cockerel crowed loudly from the top of the house.

Having told his friends the frightful story of his ordeal, the robbers never dared go back to the house. So the 'musicians' lived there in peace and harmony for the rest of their lives.

The robbers fled and the animals settled down for the night. The ass slept in the yard and the dog behind the door. The cat curled up by the fire and the cockerel settled on a beam.

Name ______________________

The elves and the shoemaker

✂

At midnight, two little elves came and sat on the shoemaker's bench stitching and tapping away. They stayed there until the job of making the shoes was finished. Then they vanished.

Again he cut out the leather in the evening and again he went to bed. In the morning, there were two pairs of beautiful shoes ready to sell, and he continued to find the shoes made up every morning. Soon the shoemaker and his wife became prosperous because many people wanted to buy the beautiful shoes.

The shoemaker cut the leather for the last pair of shoes and then he went to bed. The next morning, to his great surprise, he found the shoes made up and ready to sell. They were beautiful and he sold them quickly. Then he had enough money to buy leather for another two pairs of shoes.

The shoemaker and his wife decided to make the elves some clothes to keep them warm. They set the little clothes out on the bench one night instead of the leather. The elves put them on and danced away, full of delight. They never returned, but the shoemaker continued to prosper.

Once upon a time there lived an honest shoemaker. Both he and his wife always worked very hard, but there came the day when they only had enough leather left for one pair of shoes.

One winter evening, the shoemaker and his wife decided to hide behind a curtain to see if they could solve the mystery of who was helping them by making the shoes.

● Name ______________________________

The fisherman and his wife

✂

He hurried home to tell his wife. At once she demanded a pretty little cottage with roses round the door. Her request was granted and she was pleased.

When the fish heard her request he knew that the fisherman's wife would never be content. He turned the stone castle back into a tiny hut again and there she had to live for evermore.

Soon, however, she became dissatisfied with the house. She sent her husband to ask the fish for a stone castle. The fish granted this request and she felt very grand. For a while she was pleased.

A fisherman and his wife lived in a tiny hut by the sea. One day the fisherman caught a large fish. The fish, to his surprise, spoke saying he was an enchanted prince. The fish said he would grant favours if the fisherman would release him. So the fisherman let the fish go.

However, very soon she became dissatisfied. The cottage was not large enough and she wanted a house with a garden. The fish answered the request once more and for a while she was pleased.

Eventually, the stone castle was not enough, so the fisherman had to ask the fish to change the castle for a sparkling palace with servants. She would be the queen.

● Name ______________________________

Tutankhamun, the boy-king

● Read this passage very carefully.

The discovery of Tutankhamun's tomb in 1922 was a landmark in archaeological history. Certainly it was the most important single find in Egypt's Valley of the Kings. The tomb of the boy-king Tutankhamun had lain, unmolested by graverobbers, for more than three thousand years. The young pharaoh had died at the age of 18.

Howard Carter, funded by Lord Caernarvon, led the work of excavation. He had been searching for the burial chamber for many years. When the chamber was opened finally it was found to consist of four rooms containing caskets, vases, a golden throne, gems, clothing and weapons. Most wonderful of all was the coffin holding the mummified body of the young king.

The contents of the tomb were beyond value and explained a great deal about the life of the pharaohs of Egypt.

● Now complete the sentences below.

The tomb of the ________________ pharaoh, Tutankhamun, was discovered by ________________ ________________ in 1922. It was an amazing and ________________ discovery, for the tomb and its treasures had remained intact. In the ________________ rooms of the burial chamber there were caskets, vases and a ______________ made from ________________.

There was also some furniture, ________________ and weapons, showing what life was like in ________________ over three thousand years ago. However, the ________________ discovery of all was the golden splendour of Tutankhamun, the boy-king himself.

● Name ______________________________

The *Mary Rose*

● Read this passage very carefully.

In 1982, the Tudor flagship, The *Mary Rose*, was raised from the sea-bed, where it had lain for 437 years. This spectacular event commanded world attention. Henry VIII's famous flagship was one of the first true warships to be built.

When she sank, while sailing to attack the French fleet in 1545, the *Mary Rose* was fully manned and equipped for battle. Her discovery and her raising to the surface were very important in archaeological terms. The ship itself had been very well preserved in the silts of the Solent. In addition to this, her weapons and everyday tools and the possessions of the men who sailed her, were preserved.

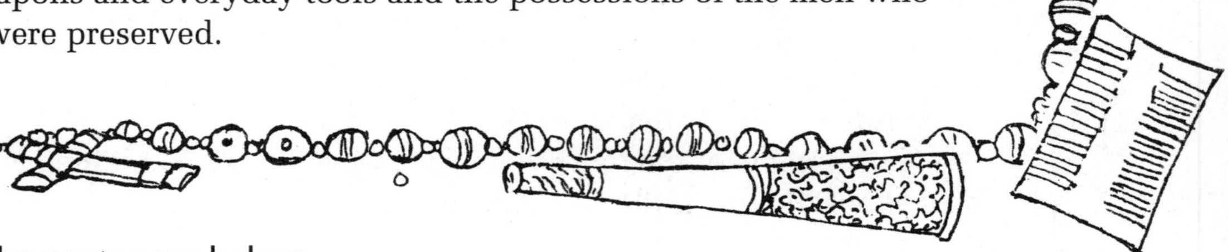

● Now complete the sentences below.

In ________________ the Tudor flagship, *Mary Rose*, was raised from the depths of the ________________ near Portsmouth harbour on the south coast of England. It had been a complicated and ________________ operation and was followed with great interest by people all over the ________________.

The *Mary Rose* ________________ in 1545 in front of King Henry ________________ and his court who were watching as the ship sailed out to meet the ________________ fleet. Seven hundred men drowned and only a few survived.

In the past there had been several attempts at salvaging the ship, but none had been ________________. At an exhibition in Portsmouth are some 2,000 of the treasures that were ________________ in the *Mary Rose*.

● Name ________________________

Spinning-tops and the gyroscope

● Read this passage very carefully.

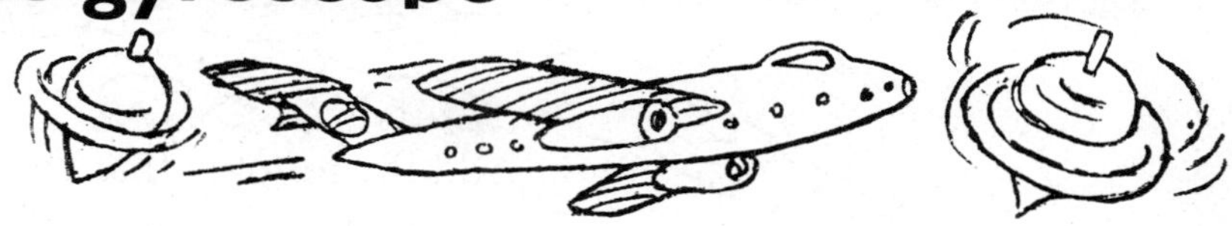

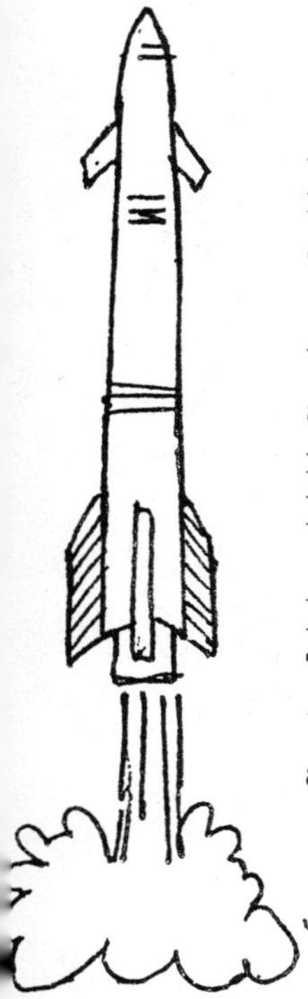

Aeroplanes fly all over the world on automatic pilot. Ships sail across oceans maintaining an even keel in rough seas. Submarines find their way round the ocean depths.

These amazing feats are the result of Elmer Ambrose Sperry's ideas. He was an American. He was watching his child play with a spinning-top in the summer of 1905. The child asked him why it stood up when it spun. It reminded him of a gyroscope, which was used in schools to demonstrate the Earth rotating on its axis.

From this principle, Sperry developed the use of the gyroscope, which keeps pointing the way it is set even when the ship is rolling and pitching. This means that the captain can keep the ship on a level and stable course. In 1908, he developed the gyrocompass which revolutionised navigation in the air and under the water.

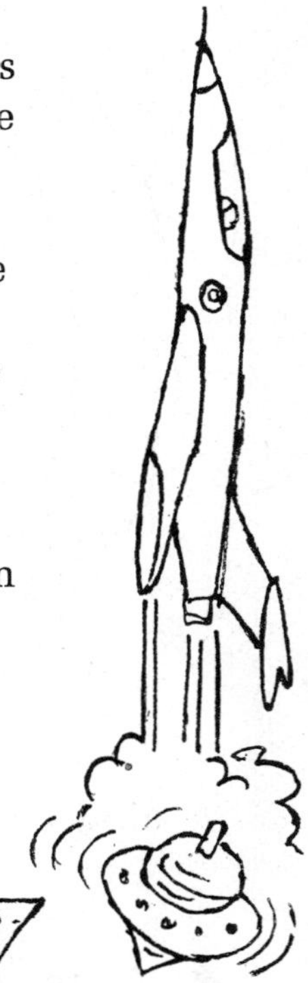

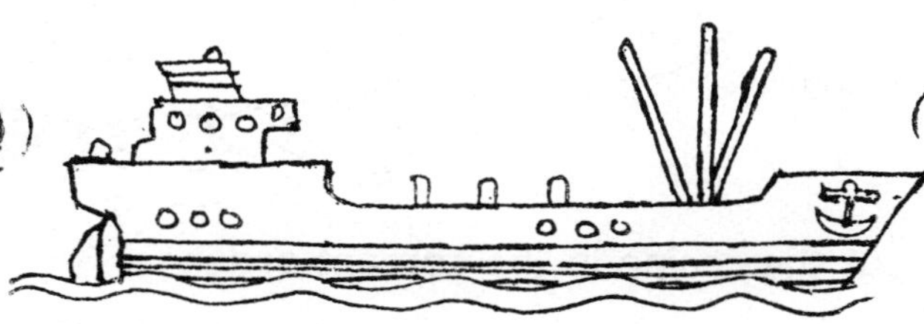

● Now complete the sentences below.

Inventions and discoveries often come from small beginnings. In ____________ Elmer Ambrose Sperry was watching his child play with a ____________ top. At this time, in schools, a ____________ was used to show how the Earth turned around on its ____________. The spinning-top reminded him of this model. As a result of these observations, Sperry was able to design an instrument which is unaffected by the ____________ of the ship. It was based on the ____________. In ____________ Sperry went on to produce the gyrocompass. This allowed precise ____________ in the air and under the water.

Name ______________________

Quick pizza

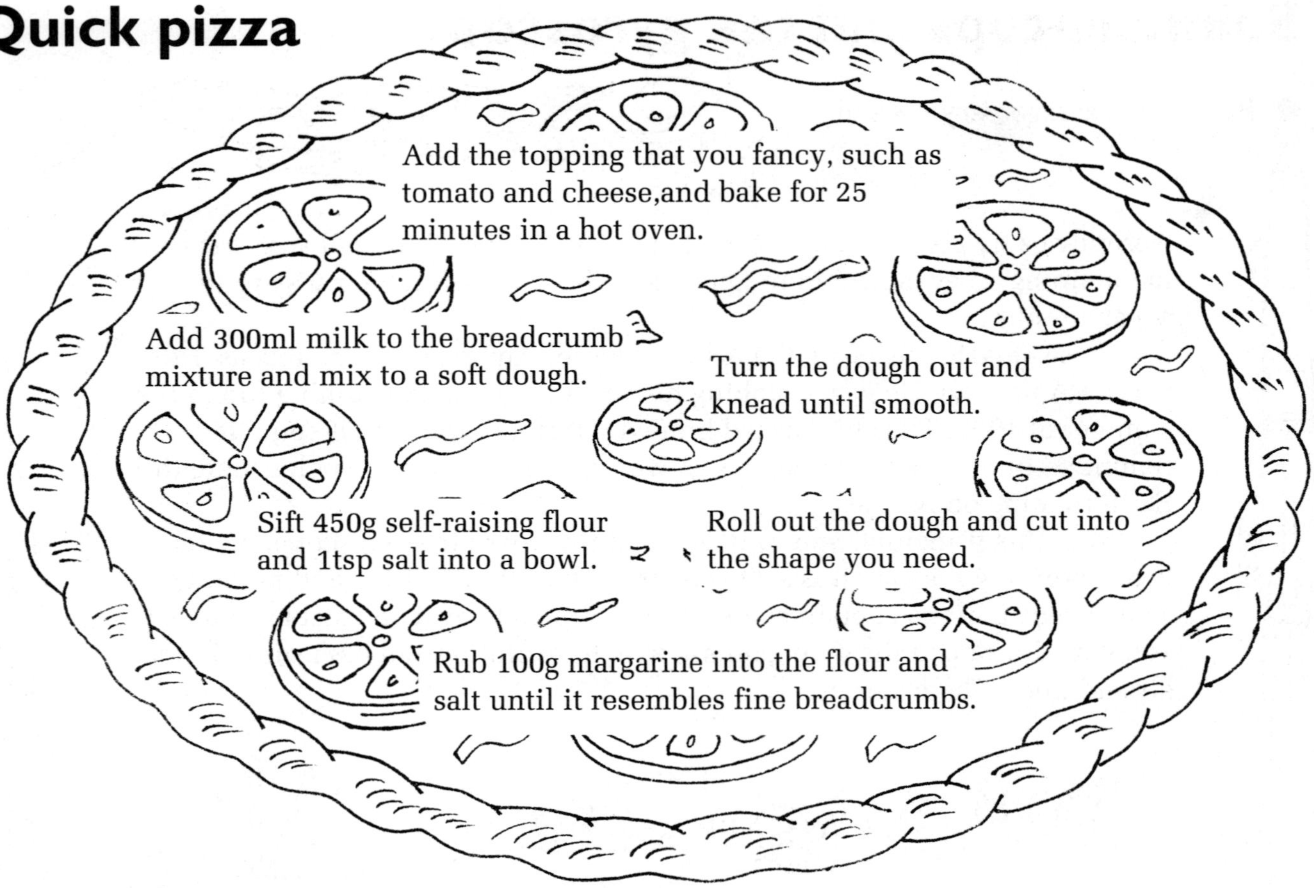

- Write out the recipe in the correct order.

1

2

3

4

5

6

● Name ______________________

Around town

- Complete this map by reading the sequence of directions below.
- Put arrows along the route you would take.

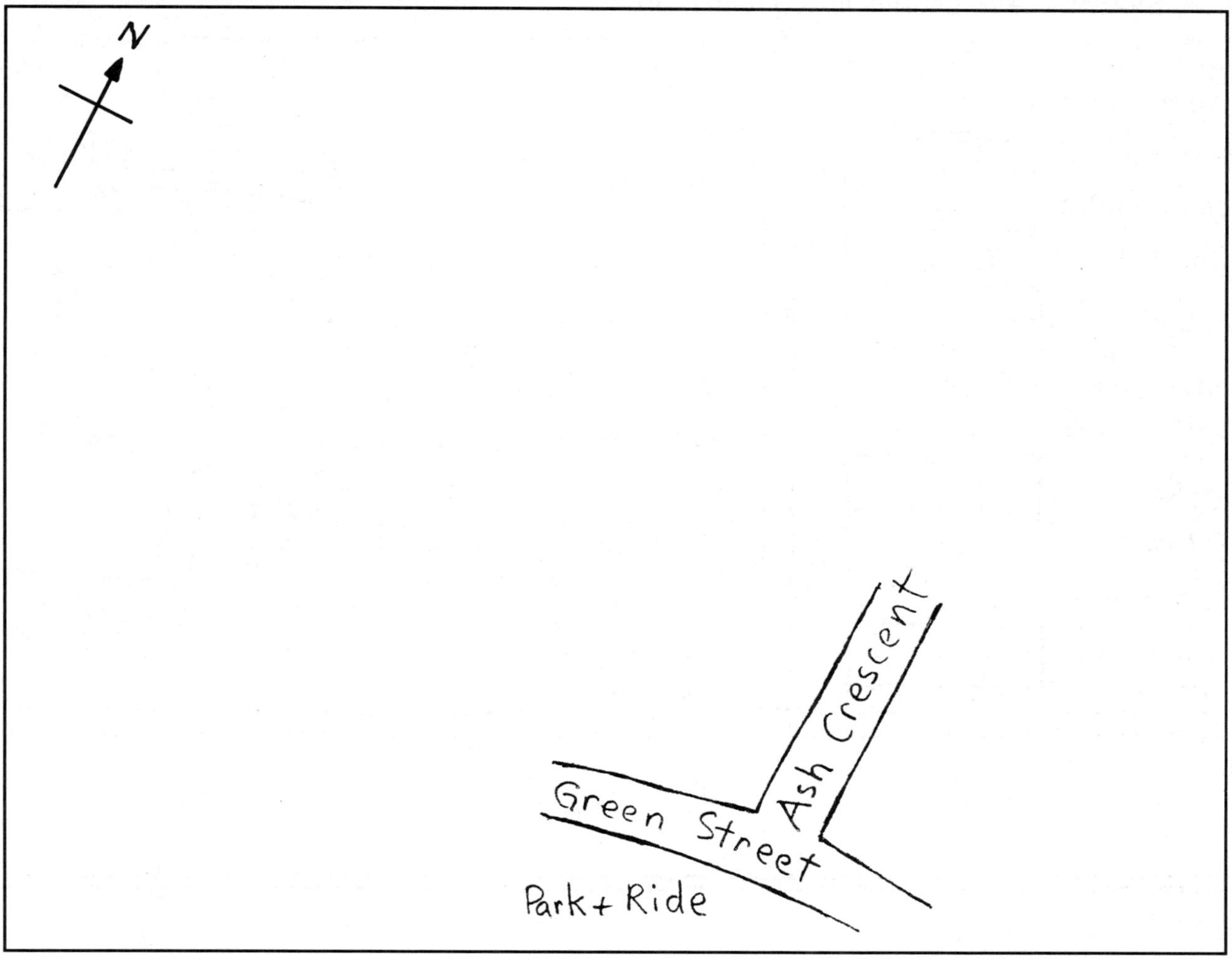

1 From the Park and Ride, catch a bus that goes west along Green Street past some trees on the left.

2 Turn right into New Street and get off at the bus stop on the left-hand side, opposite a garage.

3 Just past the garage turn right into Church Way, walking past a church with a spire on your left.

4 At the end of Church Way, turn left into Ash Crescent to go to the chemist's shop on your left.

5 Cross the road by a pedestrian crossing to a baker's shop on the opposite side of the road.

6 Follow Ash Crescent round to the south where the road joins Green Street opposite the Park and Ride.

● Name ______________________________

Around a country park

- Look at the map below.
- Imagine that you are going to meet a friend at the Museum of Folk Art. Write the directions in sequential order.

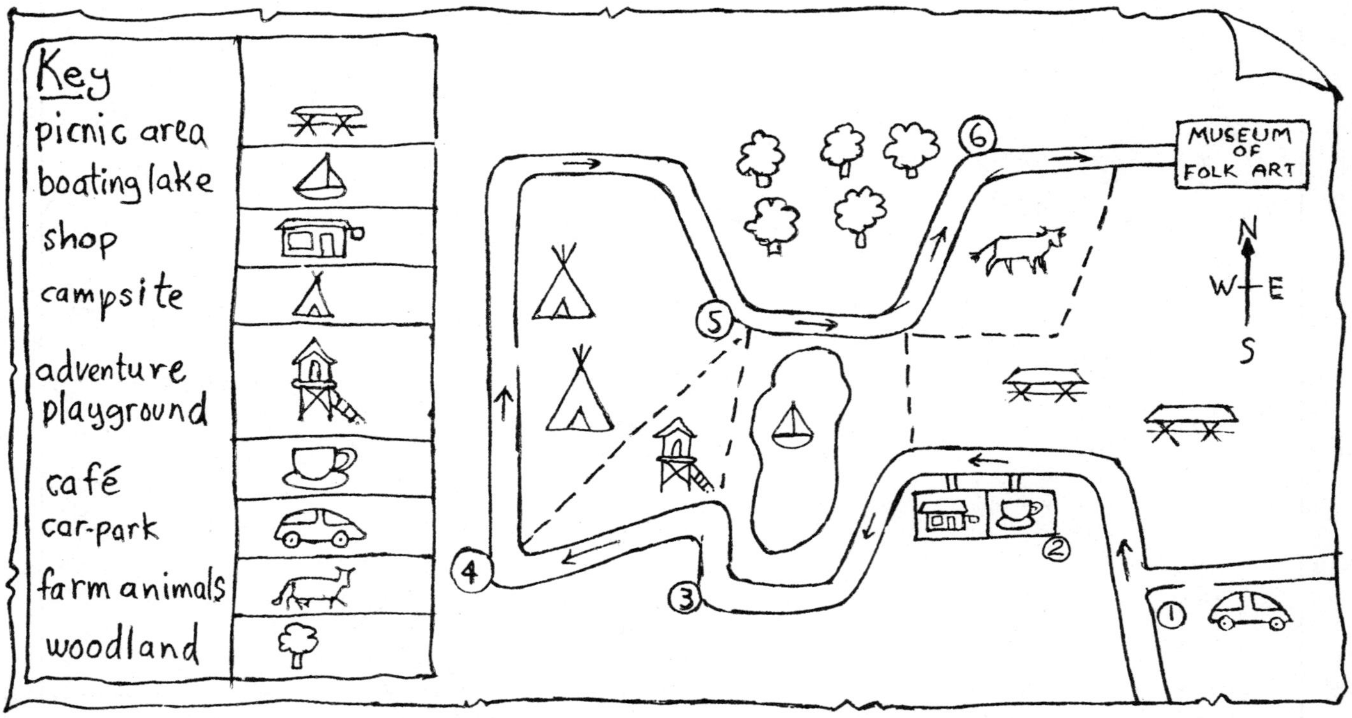

1
2
3
4
5
6

● Name ______________________________

A dog-handling competition

● Look at the diagram below.
● Write instructions for the dog handlers to follow to complete the course.

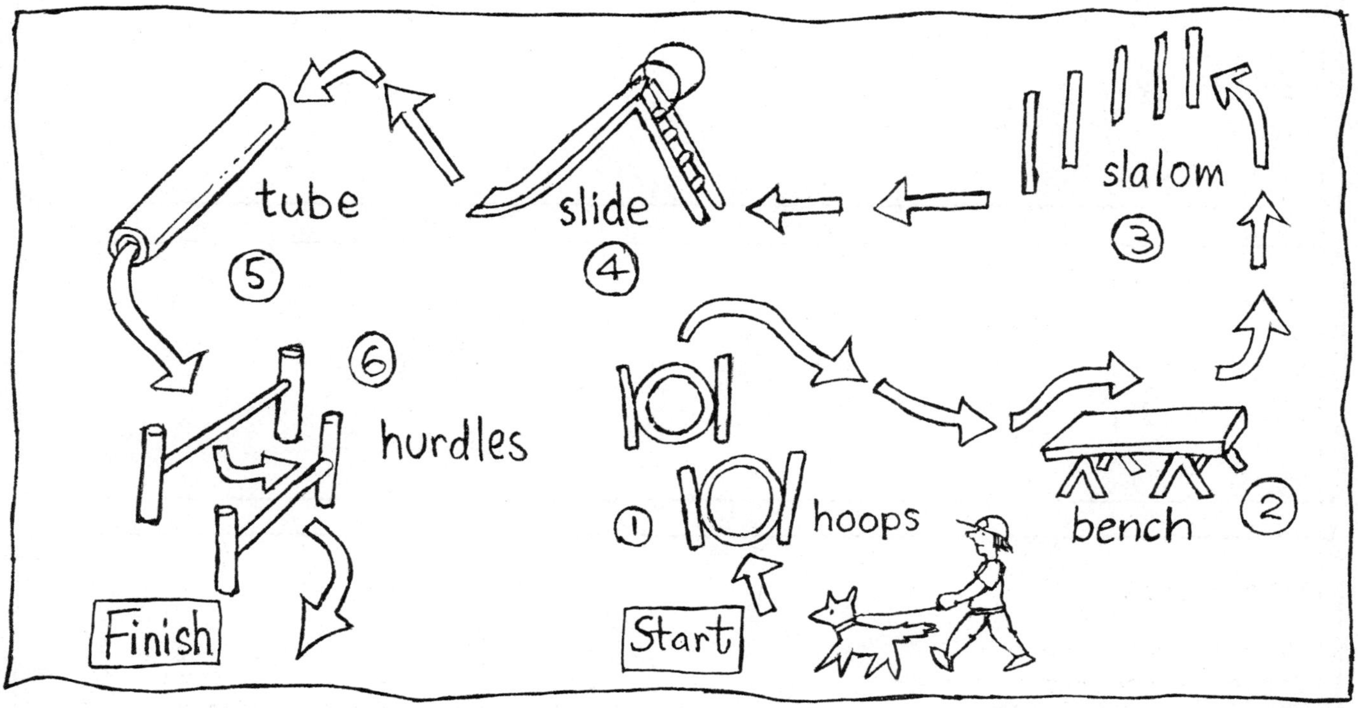

1
2
3
4
5
6

● Name ______________________________

Master sheet for sequencing activities on pages 5, 7, 9, 15, 16, 22, 23 and 24